# ABBEY THEATRE
# QUIETLY
## OWEN MCCAFFERTY

The Abbey Theatre gratefully acknowledges
the financial support of the Arts Council of
Ireland and the support of the Department
of the Arts, Heritage and the Gaeltacht.

# ABBEY THEATRE
# AMHARCLANN
# NA MAINISTREACH

THE ABBEY THEATRE is Ireland's national theatre. It was founded by W.B. Yeats and Lady Augusta Gregory. Since it first opened its doors in 1904 the theatre has played a vital and often controversial role in the literary, social and cultural life of Ireland.

We place the writer and theatre-maker at the heart of all that we do, commissioning and producing exciting new work and creating discourse and debate on the political, cultural and social issues of the day.  Our aim is to present great theatre in a national context so that the stories told on stage have a resonance with artists and audiences alike.

In 1905 the Abbey Theatre first toured internationally and continues to be an ambassador for Irish arts and culture worldwide.

Over the years, the Abbey Theatre has nurtured and premiered the work of major playwrights such as J.M. Synge and Sean O'Casey as well as contemporary classics from Sebastian Barry, Marina Carr, Bernard Farrell, Brian Friel, Thomas Kilroy, Frank McGuinness, Tom MacIntyre, Tom Murphy, Mark O'Rowe and Billy Roche.

We support a new generation of Irish writers at the Abbey Theatre including Richard Dormer, Gary Duggan, Stacey Gregg, Nancy Harris, Owen McCafferty, Elaine Murphy and Carmel Winters.

None of this can happen without our audiences and our supporters. Annie Horniman provided crucial financial support to the Abbey in its first years. Many others have followed her lead by investing in and supporting our work.

We also acknowledge the financial support of the Arts Council.

IS Í AMHARCLANN NA MAINISTREACH amharclann náisiúnta na hÉireann. W.B. Yeats agus an Bantiarna Augusta Gregory a bhunaigh í. Riamh anall ón uair a osclaíodh a doirse i 1904, ghlac an amharclann ról an-tábhachtach agus, go minic, ról a bhí sách conspóideach, i saol liteartha, sóisialta agus cultúrtha na hÉireann.

Tá an scríobhneoir agus and t-amharclannóir i gcroílár a dhéanaimid anseo san amharclann, trí shaothar nua spreagúil a choimisiúnú agus a léiriú agus trí dhioscúrsa agus díospóireacht a chruthú i dtaobh cheisteanna polaitiúla, cultúrtha agus sóisialta na linne. Is í an aidhm atá againn amharclannaíochta den scoth a láithriú i gcomhthéacs náisiúnta ionas go mbeidh dáimh ag lucht ealaíne agus lucht féachana araon leis na scéalta a bhíonn á n-aithris ar an stáitse.

I 1905 is ea a chuaigh complacht Amharclann na Mainistreach ar camchuairt idirnáisiúnta den chéad uair agus leanann sí i gcónaí de bheith ina hambasadóir ar fud an domhain d'ealaíona agus cultúr na hÉireann.

In imeacht na mblianta, rinne Amharclann na Mainistreach saothar mórdhrámadóirí ar nós J.M. Synge agus Sean O'Casey a chothú agus a chéadléiriú, mar a rinne sí freisin i gcás clasaicí comhaimseartha ó dhrámadóirí amhail Sebastian Barry, Marina Carr, Bernard Farrell, Brian Friel, Thomas Kilroy, Frank McGuinness, Tom MacIntyre, Tom Murphy, Mark O'Rowe agus Billy Roche.

Tugaimid tacaíocht chomh maith don ghlúin nua Scríbhneoirí Éireannacha in Amharclann na Mainistreach, lena n-áirítear Richard Dormer, Gary Duggan, Stacey Gregg, Nancy Harris, Owen McCafferty, Elaine Murphy agus Carmel Winters.

Ní féidir aon ní den chineál sin a thabhairt i gcrích gan ár lucht féachana agus ár lucht tacaíochta. Sholáthair Annie Horniman tacaíocht airgid ríthábhachtach don Mhainistir siar i mblianta tosaigh na hamharclainne. Lean iliomad daoine eile an dea-shampla ceannródaíochta sin uaithi ó shin trí infheistíocht a dhéanamh inár gcuid oibre agus tacaíocht a thabhairt dúinn.

Táimid fíor bhúich don tacaíocht airgeadais atá le fail ón Chomhairle Ealaíon.

# 110th Anniversary Campaign
## 1904-2014

'In the year of our 110th Anniversary, we would like to thank you for your generous support. Your investment helps us to continue to fuel the flame our founders lit over a century ago: to develop playwrights, support theatre artists and engage citizens throughout Ireland and internationally. Go raibh míle maith agat.'

*Fiach Mac Conghail, Director / Stiúrthóir*

## CORPORATE GUARDIANS

The Doyle Collection, official hotel partner of Ireland's national theatre.

  BROWN THOMAS

McCANN FITZGERALD   DIAGEO IRELAND

   ARTHUR COX

 Bank of Ireland   Northern Trust

## MEDIA PARTNERS

Sunday Independent

Irish Independent

## SUPPORTERS OF PLAYWRIGHT DEVELOPMENT

Deloitte.

### CORPORATE AMBASSADORS

Paddy Power
101 Talbot Restaurant
Bewley's
Wynn's Hotel
Abbey Travel
CRH
Conway Communications
The Merrion Hotel
Baker Tilly Ryan Glennon
National Radio Cabs
The Church Bar &
Restaurant
Clarion Consulting Limited
Manor House Hotels of
Ireland
Zero-G
Irish Poster Advertising
Bad Ass Temple Bar
DCC plc
Trocadero
Merrion Capital
J.W. Sweetman

### CORPORATE AMBASSADORS

Spector Information
Security
ely bar & brasserie
University College Cork

### CORPORATE PARTNERS

High Performance
Management

### SUPPORTING CAST

Anraí Ó Braonáin
Joe Byrne
Susan McGrath
Oonagh Desire
Róise Goan
John Daly
Zita Byrne
Kevin Walsh

### GUARDIANS OF THE ABBEY

Mrs Carmel Naughton
Sen. Fiach Mac Conghail
James McNally

### FELLOWS OF THE ABBEY

Frances Britton
Catherine Byrne
Sue Cielinski
Dónall Curtin
Tommy Gibbons
James Hickey
Dr. John Keane
Andrew Mackey
Eugene Magee
Gerard & Liv McNaughton
Donal Moore
Pat Moylan
Elizabeth Purcell Cribbin
Marie Rogan & Paul Moore
Mark Ryan
Pamela Fay

*'there's more to the truth than facts'*
– IAN

# ABBEY THEATRE
# QUIETLY
## OWEN MCCAFFERTY

### CAST (IN ORDER OF APPEARANCE)

| | |
|---|---|
| *Robert* | Robert Zawadzki |
| *Jimmy* | Patrick O'Kane |
| *Ian* | Declan Conlon |

### PRODUCTION CREDITS

| | |
|---|---|
| *Director* | Jimmy Fay |
| *Set Design* | Alyson Cummins |
| *Costume Design* | Catherine Fay |
| *Lighting Design* | Sinéad McKenna |
| *Sound Design* | Philip Stewart |
| *Voice Director* | Andrea Ainsworth |
| *Company Stage Manager* | Diarmuid O'Quigley |
| *Production Managers* | Peter Jordan & Des Kenny |
| *Casting Director* | Kelly Phelan |
| *Hair and Make-Up* | Val Sherlock |
| *Lighting Technician* | Eoin Byrne |
| *Set Construction* | Paul Manning & Vincent Bell |
| *Scenic Finishing* | Vincent Bell |
| *Sign Language Interpreter* | Vanessa O'Connell |
| *Photography* | Anthony Woods |
| *Graphic Design* | Zero-G |

*Audio described and captioned performances at the Abbey Theatre are provided by
Arts and Disability Ireland with funding from the Arts Council / An Chomhairle Ealaíon.*

# OWEN MCCAFFERTY

WRITER

QUIETLY WAS OWEN'S debut at the Abbey Theatre. It premiered on the Peacock stage in November 2012 and then toured to the Edinburgh Festival Fringe in 2013, where it won a Scotsman Fringe First Award. Owen won the 2013 Writers' Guild Award for Best Play for *Quietly*. His previous work includes *Titanic* (Scenes from the British Wreck Commissioner's Inquiry, 1912), inaugural performance at MAC, Belfast, *The Absence of Women* (Lyric Theatre, Belfast and Tricycle Theatre, London), *Days of Wine and Roses* (Donmar Theatre), *Closing Time* (National Theatre London), *Shoot The Crow* (Druid and Prime Cut Productions, Belfast) and *Scenes From The Big Picture* (National Theatre London and Prime Cut Productions, Belfast), which won the Meyer-Whitworth, John Whiting and Evening Standard Awards. Owen is the only playwright to win these three major awards in one year for the same play. Over the last 10 years many of Owen's plays have been performed throughout Europe and have won various awards.

# JIMMY FAY

### DIRECTOR

JIMMY'S PREVIOUS WORK at the Abbey Theatre includes *The Risen People*, *Quietly* (also toured to Edinburgh Festival Fringe 2013), *The Government Inspector*, *Curse of the Starving Class*, *Macbeth*, *The Playboy of the Western World*, *Ages of the Moon*, *The Resistible Rise of Arturo Ui*, *The Seafarer*, *Saved*, *The School for Scandal*, *Howie the Rookie*, *True West*, *Henry IV*, *The Muesli Belt*, *At Swim-Two-Birds*, *Melonfarmer* and *The Papar*. Jimmy spent a year as acting Literary Director of the Abbey Theatre during 2007 and 2008. Jimmy is Artistic Director of Bedrock Productions where his recent productions include *Greed*, *Colleen Bawn* (co-produced with Project Arts Centre and Civic Theatre), *This Is Our Youth*, *Roberto Zucco*, *Blasted*, *Night Just Before The Forest*, *Quay West* and *Faraway*. He was the original director of the Dublin Fringe Festival (1995-1996), which he co-founded with Bedrock Productions. He curated the theatre programme for the 2007 Kilkenny Arts Festival. Recent productions include *Mixed Marriage* (Lyric Theatre), *A Portrait of the Artist as a Young Man* (New Theatre), *The Edge of Our Bodies* (Penknife productions), *The Last Of The Red Hot Lovers* (RWCDA in Cardiff), *Happy End* (Waterford Youth Arts), *Greener*, *Between Foxrock and a Hard Place* and *The Last Days of the Celtic Tiger* (Landmark Productions), *Hoors* (Traverse Theatre) and *A Dream Play* (NAYD). Jimmy has recently been appointed the Executive Producer of the Lyric Theatre in Belfast which he takes up in May 2014.

# ALYSON CUMMINS

### SET DESIGN

ALYSON'S PREVIOUS WORK at the Abbey Theatre includes *The Risen People*, *Quietly* (also toured to Edinburgh Festival Fringe 2013), *Perve* and *No Escape*. Set and costume designs include *Summertime* (Tinderbox), *It's a Family Affair...(We'll Settle it Ourselves)* (Sherman Cymru), *How to Succeed in Business Without Really Trying* (The Company at the Lowry Salford), *Mixed Marriage* (Lyric Theatre, Belfast), *Before it Rains* (Bristol Old Vic and Sherman Cymru), *Pigeon* (Carpet Theatre), *Pornography* (Waking Exploits), *Ruben Guthrie* (IronBark), *How the World Began* (Tom Atkins at the Arcola Theatre), *The Yellow Wallpaper* (Then This Theatre), *Hamlet* (Second Age Theatre Company), *Colleen Bawn* (Project Arts Centre, Civic Theatre and Bedrock Productions), *Serious Money* and *Dying City* (Rough Magic AIB SEEDS), *Extremities* (Spark to a Flame Productions), *Crosswired* (East London Dance Festival and Shoreditch Festival), *The Trials of Brother Jero* and *Through a Film Darkly* (Arambe Productions), *Daily Bread* (Dublin Youth Theatre), *Top Girls* (Galloglass Theatre Company), *Forget me not Lane*

(The Lit Theatre Company) and *Ya Get Me* (Old Vic Education Department). Her set designs include *The Trailer of Bridget Dinnigan* (ITM) and *Off Plan* (RAW at Project Arts Centre). She was the Associate designer on *The Prince of the Pagodas* (Birmingham Royal Ballet) and *Rite of Spring / Petrushka* (Fabulous Beast). She studied Architecture at University College Dublin and after completing an internship at the Abbey Theatre, was awarded an Arts Council grant to train at Motley Theatre Design School. Alyson was a finalist in the Linbury Biennial Prize for Stage Design 2007 and completed Rough Magic's Seeds programme.

# CATHERINE FAY

COSTUME DESIGN

CATHERINE'S WORK WITH the Abbey Theatre includes *The Government Inspector, Macbeth, The Playboy of the Western World, Saved, Doubt, Doldrum Bay, Henry IV Part I* (for which she received an Irish Times/ESB Theatre Award nomination), *On Such As We* and *Chair* (Operating Theatre). Recent work includes *The Threepenny Opera* (Gate Theatre), *Carmen* (Opera Theatre Company), *Romeo and Juliet* (joint production with Corcadorca and Cork Opera House), *Dogs* (Emma Martin Dance), Winner Best Production and Best Design for ABSOLUT fringe 2012, *Body and Forgetting* and *Fast Portraits* (Liz Roche Company). She has designed much of Bedrock's back catalogue including *Wedding Day at the Cro Magnon's,*

*Roberto Zucco, Quay West, Night Just before the Forest, Wideboy Gospel* and *Massacre @ Paris*. Other work includes *It Only Ever Happens in the Movies* (National Youth Theatre), *5 Ways to Drown* (Junk Ensemble), *King Lear* (Second Age Theatre Company), *Mother Goose* and *Beauty and the Beast* (Gaiety Theatre), *Talking to Terrorists* and *Farawayan* (Calypso), *Love and Money, Pyrennes* and *Cruel and Tender* (HATCH Theatre Company), *Adrenalin* (Semper Fi), *Mushroom, The Red Hot Runaways, Antigone* and *Women in Arms* (Storytellers), *Lessness* (Gare St Lazare Players, Kilkenny Arts Festival and National Theatre, London), *Y2K Festival* (Fishamble: The New Play Company) and *Babyjane* (The Corn Exchange). Catherine is a graduate of the National College of Art and Design, Dublin.

# SINÉAD MCKENNA

LIGHTING DESIGN

SINÉAD'S WORK AT the Abbey Theatre includes *The Plough and the Stars* (2010 and 2012), *Alice in Funderland, 16 Possible Glimpses, The Burial at Thebes, Howie the Rookie* and *Finders Keepers*. Other recent work includes *Waiting for Godot* (Gare St Lazare), *Howie the Rookie, Greener, October, Last Days of the Celtic Tiger* and *Blackbird* (Landmark), *Best Man* (Everyman Productions), *Pageant* and *Swept* (Cois Ceim), *Dubliners* (The Corn Exchange), *Elevator* (THISISPOPBABY), *Travesties, The Importance of Being Earnest, Improbable Frequency* (New York Drama

Desk nomination Best Lighting Design for a Musical 2009), *The Parker Project, Life is a Dream, Attempts on Her Life* and *Dream of Autumn* (Rough Magic Theatre Company), *The Making of 'Tis Pity She's a Whore, The Lulu House* and *Medea* (Siren Productions), *The New Electric Ballroom* (Druid), *Philadelphia, Here I Come!* (Longroad), *Dancing at Lughnasa, Hamlet, A Doll's House, Macbeth, Philadelphia, Here I Come!, Othello* and *How Many Miles to Babylon?* (Second Age Theatre Company) and *Pineapple, All About Town* and *Wunderkind* (Calipo Theatre Company). Recent opera designs include *The Magic Flute* and *The Marriage of Figaro* (Opera Theatre Company), *A Midsummer Night's Dream* (Opera Ireland) and *La Traviata* (Malmo Opera House). Other theatre work includes *Private Lives* (Gate Theatre), *Honour* (b*spoke theatre company), *Henceforward* (Derby Playhouse), *Ladies and Gents* Winner Best Lighting Design Irish Times Theatre Awards 2002 (Semper Fi), *Skindeep, Scenes from a Watercooler, The Real Thing* and *Dinner with Friends* (Gúna Nua), *Candide* and *The Butterfly Ranch* (The Performance Corporation), *Macbeth, The Snow Queen* and *Merry Christmas Betty Ford* (Lyric Theatre), *Shooting Gallery* (Bedrock Productions), *The Woman who walked into Doors* (Upbeat Productions) and *Diarmaid and Grainne* (The Passion Machine). Designs for comedy include *Des Bishop, Tommy Tiernan, Neil Delamere* and *Maeve Higgins*. She is currently resident Lighting Designer at The Lir Academy.

# PHILIP STEWART
### SOUND DESIGN

PHILIP'S PREVIOUS WORK at the Abbey Theatre includes *The Risen People, Major Barbara, Quietly* (also toured to Edinburgh Festival Fringe 2013), *The House, Pygmalion, Macbeth, Ages of the Moon, Lay Me Down Softly, Terminus, A Number* and *The Big House*. As a freelance composer, he has contributed music to a broad spectrum of genres including theatre, dance, documentaries and short films. He was nominated for an Irish Times Theatre Award in 2011 for his work on *The Early Bird* (Natural Shocks). Philip studied composition at Trinity College Dublin under Donnacha Dennehy and Roger Doyle.

# DECLAN CONLON

IAN

DECLAN'S PREVIOUS WORK at the Abbey Theatre includes *The Hanging Gardens*, *Drum Belly*, *Quietly* (also toured to Edinburgh Festival Fringe 2013), *The House*, Winner Irish Times Theatre Award for Best Actor 2012, *Terminus* (National and International tour), Manchester Theatre Awards nomination for Best Actor 2011, *The Last Days of a Reluctant Tyrant*, *A Whistle in the Dark*, *Famine*, *The Patriot Game*, *The Burial at Thebes*, *The Crucible*, *The Recruiting Officer*, *Julius Caesar*, *A Month in The Country*, Winner Irish Times Theatre Award for Best Supporting Actor 2006, *True West*, *The Hamlet Project*, *All My Sons*, *Henry IV* (Part 1), *Heavenly Bodies*, *What Happened Bridgie Cleary*, and *The Last Ones*. Other theatre work includes *An Enemy of the People*, *The Last Summer*, *The Book of Evidence* (originally produced in conjunction with Kilkenny Arts Festival) and *The Importance of Being Earnest* (Gate Theatre), *Juno and the Paycock* (Gaiety Theatre), *The Sanctuary Lamp* (b*spoke theatre company), *Improbable Frequency* and *Copenhagen*, Irish Times Theatre Award nomination for Best Actor 2002 (Rough Magic Theatre Company), *Freefall* and *Cat on a Hot Tin Roof* (Corn Exchange), *Miss Julie*, *Greener* and *The Secret Garden* (Landmark Productions), *The Country* (Arclight Productions), *As You Like It*, *The Spanish Tragedy*, *La Lupa*, *The Mysteries* and *Henry VI* (Royal Shakespeare Company), *The Walls*, *The Ends of the Earth* and *The Machine Wreckers* (National Theatre, London), *Macbeth* (West End), *Our Country's Good* (Out Of Joint at the Young Vic and UK tour) and *Uncle Vanya* (Lyric Theatre, Belfast). Television work includes *The Tudors* (Showtime), *Fair City*, *Amber*, *Raw*, *Trouble in Paradise*, *Proof* and *Bachelors Walk* (RTÉ), *Single Handed* (RTÉ and ITV), *Anytime Now*, *Dangerfield* and *The Family* (BBC) and *Cromwell* (Title Films). Film credits include *Love Eternal*, *Calvary*, *Basket Case*, *Debris*, *Hereafter*, *The Trouble with Sex*, *Honest*, *All Souls Day* and *Roman Spring of Mrs Stone*. Radio work includes *The Burial at Thebes* and *The Hounds of the Baskerville*.

# PATRICK O'KANE

JIMMY

PATRICK WON THE Best Actor award at The Stage Awards for Acting Excellence for his performance in *Quietly* at the Edinburgh Festival Fringe 2013. His previous work with the Abbey Theatre includes *16 Possible Glimpses*, *Medea*, *The House* (2000), *Observe the Sons of Ulster Marching Towards the Somme*, *The Plough and the Stars*, *Hamlet* and *As The Beast Sleeps*, Irish Times/ESB Award for Best Supporting Actor 1999. Other theatre work includes *The Crucible* and *Cat on a Hot Tin Roof* (Lyric Theatre, Belfast) *Ashes to Ashes* and *Cold Comfort* (Prime Cut Productions), *Popcorn* (Nottingham Playhouse, West Yorkshire Playhouse and West End), *War Horse*, *Scenes From The*

*Big Picture, Closing Time, The Playboy of the Western World, Peer Gynt* and *Romeo and Juliet* (National Theatre, London), *Macbeth* (Royal Shakespeare Company), *Dr Faustus, A Whistle in The Dark, Shoot the Crow, Unidentified Human Remains and The True Nature of Love, Julius Caesar, Miss Julie* and *Donny Boy* (Royal Exchange), *Sweet Bird of Youth, Edward II, Lulu* and *1953* (Citizens Theatre, Glasgow), *Titanic* (MAC, Belfast), *The Crucible* (Regent's Park Open Air Theatre), *Volunteers* (Gate Theatre), *The Strip and Trust* (Royal Court) and *The Postman Always Rings Twice* (West Yorkshire Playhouse). Patrick has also been an Associate Artist with Nottingham Playhouse and with Prime Cut Productions where he directed *The Trestle at Pope Lick Creek*. Film and television work includes *Prometheus* (Brandywine Productions), *Perkins 14* (After Dark Films), *Exorcist – The Beginnings* (Morgan Creek Productions), *Charlotte's Red* (4 x 4 Productions), *Stealing Rembrandt* (Fine & Mellow Productions), *Octane* (Delux Productions), *Jamaica Inn* (Origin Pictures), *Strike Back* and *Game of Thrones* (HBO), *The Borgias* (LB Productions), *The Fall, New Tricks, Holby Blue, Five Days, Waking The Dead, Holby City, Holy Cross, A Rap At The Door* and *As The Beast Sleeps* (BBC), *Any Time Now* (Comet Productions), *Gunpowder, Treason* and *Plot* (Raging Star Films), *Wire In The Blood* (ITV Productions). Patrick is a NESTA Fellow and his book *Actors' Voices* is published by Oberon Books.

# ROBERT ZAWADZKI

### ROBERT

QUIETLY IS ROBERT'S debut at the Abbey Theatre. Robert trained at the National Theatre School of Poland in Wroclaw. Theatre work includes *The Forefathers, Marat Sade* and *Burning Russia* (Modjeska Theatre Legnica), *Malambo the Blacksmith* (Drama Laboratory, Warsaw), *The Shoemakers* (Baltic Dramatic Theatre, Koszalin). Robert has collaborated with numerous Polish Theatres including Na Woli Theatre, Warsaw; Studio Theatre, Warsaw; InVitro Pre-Premiere Stage, Lublin; Baltic Dramatic Theatre, Koszalin; Dramatic Theatre, Opole; Polish Theatre, Bielsko-Biała and independent Street Theatre Group 'Asocjacja 2006', Poznan. Robert was honoured in the 'On the Top' category in the Best Polish Theatre Actors Awards in 2010. He made his debut as a director in 2012 with *Games in the Backyard* (Dramatic Theatre, Opole). Film credits include *Anna and Modern Day Slavery* (2012), *Der Sündenfall: Teil 1 der Trylogie – Weltenbrand* (2012) *Within the Whirlwind* (2010), *Wenecja* (2010), *My Big Fat Moonie Wedding* (2007) and *The Pianist* (2002). Robert has also appeared in a several TV Shows including *Murphy's Law* (BBC), *Pierwsza Milosc* (known in Ireland as *Soupy Norman*), *Czas honoru, Niania, Na Wspolnej, Samo Zycie, Teraz albo nigdy, Ojciec Mateusz* and *Prawo Agaty*.

# Abbey Theatre
# Staff & Supporters

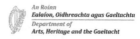

The Abbey Theatre gratefully acknowledges the financial support of the Arts Council / An Chomhairle Ealaíon and the support of the Department of the Arts, Heritage and the Gaeltacht.

Archive partner of the Abbey Theatre.

# Quietly

*Quietly* marks Owen McCafferty's debut at the Abbey Theatre. Over the last twenty years his plays have been performed throughout Europe and have won various awards. Previous work includes *Titanic* (*Scenes from the British Wreck Commissioner's Inquiry, 1912*), the inaugural performance at MAC, Belfast; *The Absence of Women* (Lyric Theatre, Belfast, and Tricycle Theatre, London); *Days of Wine and Roses* (Donmar Theatre); *Closing Time* (National Theatre, London); *Shoot the Crow* (Druid and Prime Cut Productions, Belfast); *Mojo Mickybo* (Kabosh); and *Scenes from the Big Picture* (National Theatre, London, and Prime Cut Productions, Belfast), which won the Meyer-Whitworth, John Whiting and *Evening Standard* Awards. He is the only playwright to win these three major awards in one year for the same play. He is an Artistic Associate of Prime Cut Productions.

OWEN McCAFFERTY

# Quietly

ff

FABER & FABER

First published in 2012
by Faber and Faber Limited
74–77 Great Russell Street
London WC1B 3DA

Reprinted 2014

Typeset by Country Setting, Kingsdown, Kent CT14 8ES
Printed in England by CPI Group (UK) Ltd, Croydon, CRO 4YY

ISBN 978-0-571-29943-0

FSC
www.fsc.org
MIX
Paper from
responsible sources
FSC® C101712

4 6 8 10 9 7 5 3

*Nothing much has changed*
*It's mostly still the same*
*The cold sun shines through rain*
*And yet Belfast is born again*

Foy Vance
'Belfast Is Born Again'

# Characters

**Robert**
Polish, thirty-four

**Jimmy**
fifty-two

**Ian**
fifty-two

*The characters in this play
both the living and the dead
are fictional*

QUIETLY

*The stage is in darkness. Lights up.*

*A bar in Belfast, 2009. Northern Ireland are playing Poland in a World Cup qualifier on a big screen TV.*

*Robert is playing the poker machine. He receives a text message.*

i can't live like this

i'm not happy either

do u luv me

of course i do

then what

i don't know

i'm feel alone – what am i doing here – i want to go back to poland

can't talk now the place is starting to fill up

i need u

talk later

**Robert**      fuckin torture – she wanted to be here – begged me – i didn't force her – fuckin made it happen that's what i did – and what – this shit

*He moves behind the bar and watches the match.*

*Jimmy enters.*

|  | alright jimmy – late tonight – second half just started – two one up to yous – evans just scored – not over yet though |
| --- | --- |
| Jimmy | aye – was thinkin about not comin at all – but then i've somethin to do so here i am |
| Robert | pint is it |
| Jimmy | i'll try one an see how that goes – a few kids outside on the cider – they give you any grief |
| Robert | no it's fine |
| Jimmy | do you want me to go out and get rid of them |
| Robert | no i don't want any trouble |
| Jimmy | sometimes that's what's called for |
| Robert | they're only kids |
| Jimmy | kids can do more damage than you think |

*Robert serves Jimmy his drink and opens a bottle of Coke for himself. They both say cheers in Polish. They watch the match. Robert sends a text message.*

u watching the match

no – putting the baby to bed

kiss him for me

what's the score

2-1 to yous – jammie bastards

up yer polish hole

up yer nordie hole

any trouble on the way to work

no

get a taxi home

maybe

he's crying – talk later

**Robert**    yes yes yes – shit – who was it

**Jimmy**    don't know

**Robert**    jelen is it

**Jimmy**    never heard of him – make no difference

**Robert**    come on poland – come on poland

**Jimmy**    fuck poland – what do you care anyway –
you loved the place so much ya left it
behind – this is home now – the lovely
belfast

**Robert**    not that you'd know anything about it but
it's in my heart

**Jimmy**    how would a not know about that

**Robert**    i've left nothing behind – it's there – i carry
it with me

**Jimmy**    you should support northern

**Robert**    fuck northern ireland – do you support
them

**Jimmy**    not really – but then this place probably
hasn't looked after me as well as it's
looked after you

**Robert**    yeah i'm livin the dream baby

**Jimmy**    who scored your goal

**Robert**    jelen

| Jimmy | still never heard of him |
| --- | --- |
| Robert | you know a lot about polish football do you |
| Jimmy | a know a bit |
| Robert | you know nothing – this place doesn't know the rest of the world exists |
| Jimmy | is that right |
| Robert | so what bit do you know then |
| Jimmy | the nineteen seventy-four world cup – i know that bit |
| Robert | the nineteen seventy-four world cup – bullshit |
| Jimmy | the golden boot – grzegorz lato – poland – seven goals – and joint second with neeskens from holland with five was – andrzej szarmach – poland came third in that world cup – an who did the beat in the play off for third place – the mighty brazil – one-nil on the sixth of july nineteen seventy-four |
| Robert | how do you know all that – you learn it off for a quiz |
| Jimmy | don't do quizzes – doesn't matter how i know it – an another thing too – who did poland stop from even gettin to the world cup finals |
| Robert | northern ireland |
| Jimmy | no fuck – england – can't remember the score – might have been one-nil not sure |

| | |
|---|---|
| Robert | we've no chance of getting to this world cup |
| Jimmy | a wouldn't know |
| Robert | how do you not know you sit and watch all the matches |
| Jimmy | sit here an have a pint but i don't really watch them |
| | *Robert receives a text.* |
| | poker after work ? |
| | can't |
| | what about the money u owe me – i want my money |
| | i'm good for it |
| | tomorrow |
| Robert | what's the point in scoring a goal then playing like headless chickens |
| Jimmy | if the could stop themselves from playin like that do ya not think they'd do it |
| Robert | it wasn't a question |
| Jimmy | right – sounded like one |
| Robert | did you hear the news |
| Jimmy | not interested in news |
| Robert | there was trouble earlier on |
| Jimmy | between us an the poles |
| Robert | us – i thought you didn't support them |
| Jimmy | like it or not it's still us |

| | |
|---|---|
| Robert | smashed up some pub in the city centre – i was thinking maybe i should put the shutters up on the windows |
| Jimmy | should be alright – only wee lads hangin about out there – not even at the match – no interest in it – just messin |
| Robert | it'll be alright then |
| Jimmy | certainly – i'm here anyway – (*Pause.*) – there's a man comin in later on to see me – he wants to talk with me – there might be a bit a trouble with him – but it's nothin for you to worry about |
| Robert | no trouble – can't afford for trouble – i get the blame |
| Jimmy | all a meant was just in case there was a bit a shoutin – don't panic |
| Robert | a bit of shouting |
| Jimmy | yes a bit a shoutin – nothin for you to get involved in – ya understan – stay out of it – nothin to do with you |
| Robert | a bit of shouting – everyone shouts here – it's the national sport |
| Jimmy | we all need to be heard at the same time |
| Robert | smashed a pub up in town – not sure who started it – could be us – a lot of football hooligans back home – right wing – madmen – cross the fucking ball – people paid to cross the ball and they can't cross the fucking thing |
| Jimmy | my mother used to say you'd think with all the money they earned they'd be able to kick the ball properly |

| | |
|---|---|
| **Robert** | she follow football |
| **Jimmy** | no – hated it |
| **Robert** | hated it |
| **Jimmy** | yes hated it |
| **Robert** | why |
| **Jimmy** | what were you back in poland a policeman |
| **Robert** | a barman |
| **Jimmy** | barman – a fuckin barman |
| **Robert** | yeah |
| **Jimmy** | why haven't ya got the hang of it then |
| **Robert** | you don't need to be any good to serve you pints of piss |
| **Jimmy** | polish beer any better |
| **Robert** | dog piss would be better |
| **Jimmy** | do ya drink much dog piss in poland |
| **Robert** | enough |
| **Jimmy** | get some polish beer in an i'll try it |
| **Robert** | right |
| **Jimmy** | a will |
| **Robert** | right |
| **Jimmy** | so you were a barman in poland and ya came over here to be a barman |
| **Robert** | i didn't come over here to be a barman – belfast isn't barman mecca – not the fucking capital of the barman world – i came over to work and ended up a barman because i was one before |

| Jimmy | more money here – peace process – when i was a kid no one came here – only people in belfast were belfast people – an british soldiers – the only black men here had uniforms on them |
|---|---|
| Robert | money used to be great not so great now – why'd your mother hate football |
| Jimmy | who knows she just did |
| Robert | watching this rubbish i'm starting to hate it too |
| Jimmy | anybody ya know over for the match |
| Robert | no – everybody i know is already here – shoot you stupid fuck |
| Jimmy | would you go back |
| Robert | maybe |
| Jimmy | not like it here |
| Robert | don't know |
| Jimmy | we're not very good with foreigners |
| Robert | you always live in belfast then |
| Jimmy | all my days – never left – belfast man through an through |
| Robert | you should travel |
| Jimmy | fuck travel |
| Robert | come to poland – watch northern ireland play there |
| Jimmy | what the fuck would a want to do that for |
| Robert | see where i live – you might like it – you might want to stay there |

| | |
|---|---|
| Jimmy | if it's so good why didn't you stay there |
| Robert | good save – your keeper's good – who is he |
| Jimmy | taylor a think ya call him – don't know who he plays for like |
| Robert | our keeper's a dickhead |
| Jimmy | put another pint on there |

*Robert pulls him a pint.*

when do you have a drink

| | |
|---|---|
| Robert | i don't |
| Jimmy | not ever |
| Robert | no |
| Jimmy | worked behind a bar seen it all |
| Robert | no – both my parents were alcoholics – frightened to take one |
| Jimmy | i can see how that would be right – it never really affected me – a few pints an that's me |
| Robert | they lived a life of no money so they drank |
| Jimmy | easy enough done |
| Robert | doesn't have to be that way |
| Jimmy | both dead are the |
| Robert | no – both back in poland |
| Jimmy | you send them money back |
| Robert | no |
| Jimmy | right |

*They watch the match.*

**Robert**   jesus christ

**Jimmy**   if someone didn't know anythin about football an ya were to describe it to them – an then the watch this match – the wouldn't realise the were watchin football would the

**Robert**   no

**Jimmy**   what would it look like the were watchin

**Robert**   a fuck-up

**Jimmy**   correct – a fuck-up – ya ever play football

**Robert**   no – still do better than these clowns – you ever play it

**Jimmy**   only as a wee lad at the bottom of the street – used to play matches to the best of twenty – took hours sometimes

**Robert**   the best of twenty take days here

**Jimmy**   aye

**Robert**   you look as if you were useless

**Jimmy**   how can ya tell

**Robert**   the way you walk

**Jimmy**   the way i walk – you talk a lot a balls – kneecapped – long after a played football

**Robert**   kneecapped

**Jimmy**   shot through the knees – for nothing – robbed a sweetie shop when i was seventeen – well for something but it was nothing – robbed a sweet shop when i was about seventeen – stupid – yer right about the football though i was rubbish – plenty of energy but no skill – used to annoy the other kids – just got in the way of things most a the time

*Ian enters.*

**Robert**   fuck me – own goal – three-one

**Jimmy**   (*to Robert*)
remember what a said – this has nothing to do with you

**Robert**   yeah yeah yeah – fuck

**Ian**   my name is ian . . .

*Jimmy head-butts Ian. He holds Robert in place with his stare.*

(*To Robert.*) it's fine – ya understand – it's fine
(*To Jimmy.*) – that it – that the only reason you agreed to see me

**Jimmy**   yes

**Ian**   i think you want more than that

**Jimmy**   right – i need you to understan somethin – the head-butt was just an indication ya understand – it's not out a character either – i'll kick you all over the fuckin street – the only thing stopping me doin that – at the moment – is the fact that a wouldn't stop until ya had no fuckin head left

**Ian**   (*to Robert*)
two pints of harp please

| | |
|---|---|
| Robert | you all drink harp – harp is dog piss – should drink good polish beer |
| Ian | i'm not askin you to drink it am a |
| Robert | ok – two pints |
| Jimmy | you expectin someone else |
| Ian | no |
| Jimmy | ask me do i want a pint a harp |
| Ian | do you want a pint of harp |
| Jimmy | i want fuck all from you |
| Robert | just the one then |
| Ian | i ordered two – just set them on the counter |
| Robert | you watch the football |
| Ian | not really |
| Robert | nobody watch the football – nobody support their country |
| Ian | who's playin |
| Robert | northern ireland and poland – not very good |
| Ian | you polish |
| Robert | yes polish |
| Ian | is that why there was trouble in town because a the match |
| Robert | the match is an excuse maybe |
| Ian | maybe |

| | |
|---|---|
| **Jimmy** | (*to Ian*)<br>stop talkin to him – right – stop fuckin talkin to him as if yer havin some type a social fuckin thing – (*To Robert.*) – watch the match – this has fuck all to do with you so just watch the match |
| **Robert** | alright – pass the fucking ball – jesus christ – poles are dickheads |

*They watch the match.*

| | |
|---|---|
| **Ian** | do you want to know why i'm here |
| **Jimmy** | oh i know why you're fuckin here – although i'm hopin it's cancer – cancer of somethin that's a real fuck-up – the eyeballs or the dick or somethin – somethin that takes its time to rot – please tell me it's cancer – an that ya need to get into heaven because you're really a good person – i knew this man once – dead now – this man married his childhood sweetheart – lovely girl – in love the two a them – all that type a gear – had kids – four a think – he had a good enough job an that – sold cars – married for about thirty years – and throughout the whole time he had affairs with other women – personally speakin i don't really give a fuck about things like that – it's his life i don't care – he gets cancer – riddled with it – terminal – this fucker's lyin on his deathbed an he wants to get into heaven – big catholic by the way – not that that matters – now here's this poor woman thinkin for thirty years she's been in a lovin carin relationship with a man that |

was faithful to her – on his deathbed this fucker says i've been havin affairs for thirty years dear – please forgive me – no moral fuckin fibre – frightened of dyin an couldn't keep his pain to himself the fucker – he had to offload it on to her didn't he – out of all the people i know – an a didn't even know him that well – i hate that fucker the most

Ian       i haven't got cancer – i don't believe in god – we're the same age

Jimmy    you an god – fuck me

Ian       me an you

Jimmy    fuck what age we are

Ian       i'm here because we're the same age

Jimmy    you're not my fuckin age – my age has to do with the life i've led – you haven't led my life

Ian       i led a life – my life

Jimmy    i don't fuckin care – (*To Robert.*) – a pint of dog piss please – score predictions – what are they

Robert   three-one now – about thirty minutes to go – difficult – are we betting on this

Jimmy    no – i'll make it easy for ya – poland are shite

Robert   so are northern ireland

Jimmy    less shite

Ian       we were both sixteen an now we're both fifty-two

| | |
|---|---|
| **Jimmy** | we're predicting scores at the moment – as far as i know age has got fuck all to do with that |
| **Ian** | it means something |
| **Jimmy** | three-two to northern ireland |
| **Robert** | four-three to poland |
| **Jimmy** | that's not predictin the score that's just hopin for a result |
| **Robert** | ok i'll think harder about it – four-three to poland |
| **Jimmy** | up yer polish hole |
| **Robert** | up your nordie hole |
| **Jimmy** | (*to Ian*)<br>you ever watch poland play before |
| **Ian** | no |
| **Jimmy** | sure – not even the second half of a match – too busy to watch the first half but catch the second |
| **Ian** | no |
| **Jimmy** | no |
| | *Ian starts into his second pint. They watch the match.* |
| | this is shite turn it off |
| **Robert** | turn it off – what is that turn it off |
| **Jimmy** | it's shite |
| **Robert** | it's meant to be shite |

| | |
|---|---|
| **Jimmy** | (*to Ian*)<br>all the others refuse did the – not want to<br>hear yer sad little story – am i your last<br>hope a salvation |
| **Ian** | you're the first |
| **Jimmy** | i should feel privileged |
| **Ian** | it's because we're the same age |
| **Jimmy** | stop fucking saying that – nothing to do<br>with age |
| **Ian** | ya must want to say somethin or ya<br>wouldn't have agreed to meet me |
| **Jimmy** | i pick when i want to speak |
| **Ian** | and where |
| **Jimmy** | you have a problem with here |
| **Ian** | no – i understand why – doesn't make it<br>any easier – but that's the point |
| **Jimmy** | is it |
| **Ian** | yes – i've been here before – recently |
| **Jimmy** | had a look an then moved on |
| **Ian** | yes |
| **Jimmy** | how long did you look for |
| **Ian** | two hours – stood across the road |
| **Jimmy** | what time of day was it |
| **Ian** | about tea time |
| **Jimmy** | right – should've called in and said hello |
| **Ian** | stood there for two hours |

| | |
|---|---|
| Jimmy | there was flesh stuck to the wall across the road – where you were standin – difficult to scrape off – difficult because it's flesh an you don't want to scrape it off |
| Ian | you drink here aye |
| Jimmy | i watch football here |
| Ian | i drink in town |
| Jimmy | how interestin |
| Ian | on my own – a few pints – ya know |
| Jimmy | is that it – have we shared now – bonded – are we now soul mates – can we confide – have you tried to top yourself and failed – is that why you're here |
| Ian | i'm here because you agreed to meet me |
| Jimmy | fifty-two – took a long time to ask |
| Ian | it needed to be done |
| Jimmy | well fuckin bully for you |
| Ian | can we assume somethin |
| Jimmy | yeah let's do that – let's assume – i assume you're a cunt |
| Ian | let's assume we can both kick each other round the street |

*Jimmy stands up. Ian stands up. They face each other. The moment lasts, then they sit down.*

the truth is i don't know why i'm here – i feel dislocated or something – i have to

|  | sort things out – not being able to look myself in the eye when i'm havin a shave maybe – that's why i'm here |
|---|---|
| Jimmy | you're here because i allowed you to be here |
| Ian | what we do then is up to you |
| Jimmy | is it |
| Ian | yes |
| Jimmy | maybe you should sit there an drink yer pint – take yer surroundings in – watch the match – if talk happens it happens – if it doesn't – well sure ya had a pint an ya watched a match |

*They watch the match.*

|  | poland is ninety-nine per cent catholic – that's a lot of catholics isn't it – do some damage there – every time you shook a stick you'd hit one – (*To Robert.*) – anyone ever hit you with a stick robert |
|---|---|
| Robert | my father – many times |
| Jimmy | did he |
| Robert | yes |
| Jimmy | fuck that – my father never lifted his hand to me in his life – he should've done |
| Robert | you wanted your father to hit you – been hit like me you wouldn't say that |
| Jimmy | what would a want someone to fuckin hit me for – whenever i was a kid and a did somethin ya got slapped for my mother |

used to do the slappin – he should've
helped her out with that – taken the heat
off her ya know

**Robert**     not slapped – beaten

**Jimmy**     men can be full a rage

**Robert**     that's no excuse

**Jimmy**     no – if he were here now i might get him to
slap me – it wasn't in him – when i was a
kid a beat another wee lad up – a
remember the look of disappointment on
my da's face when he found out – i was
right in doing it though – wee bastard
thought he was bein smart – round here
when i grew up was mixed – i said to ya –
we used to play football at the bottom a
the street – sometimes the ball would get
hit into the river – if it didn't go too far
out the tide would push it back in – ya
kicked it too far out and it just floated off
– there was a wee lad a few years older than
me – a protestant – we were only kids but
he started wearing a tartan scarf – my dad
had bought me a new football – so i
brought it down to the bottom a the street
– yer wee man kicked it into the river as
hard as he could – i beat the fuck out of
him – i was smackin his head off the
pavement – only the other wee lads pulled
me off i'd have killed the wee fucker – see
when i was doin it too – i was screaming in
his face – fuckin orange bastard – it came
out a nowhere – fuckin orange bastard –
fuckin orange bastard – fuckin – orange –
bastard – (*To Ian.*) – there ya go – yer

turn – i've paved the way for ya – you were right to do what you did – i've decided to make it easier for you – this is me playin my part in the truth and reconciliation process – you were right – we were all cunts – all of us – all the catholics – even the ninety-nine per cent in poland – and the ones tearin up belfast today

Ian            can we do this in private

Jimmy          no

Ian            it should be in private

Jimmy          i think it should be open – if this succeeds we will be seen as the first – we will be held up as a beacon – a fuckin nobel prize maybe – robert will be our committee – our truth an reconciliation committee – won't you robert

Robert         i'm watching the match

Jimmy          perfect – i'm sure you already know robert but i think i should explain the background to this – for thirty-odd years this was a fucked up place – blah blah blah – now it's not such a fucked up place – it's the love-in capital of europe

Robert         love-in capital of europe – yeah i can see that

Jimmy          yes – you know what losing your bottle means

Robert         no

| | |
|---|---|
| **Jimmy** | when you lose your bottle you have no courage for the fight – politicians here have lost – if they ever had it – their courage for the fight – the fight being a truthful and honest look at ourselves – now you may think that doesn't matter because it is indeed the way of the world – but with here you see it feels like we have been given the opportunity to examine ourselves – to come to a conclusion – to get to the end – however the powers-that-be don't want that because they might find out who they really are – and what fucking right minded person wants that – you might have to examine all types of shite then – which brings me to the truth and reconciliation committee – we have been told we are not ready for that – not mature enough – and as always each little vested interest says it would only work if everyone was truthful – and again who the fuck wants that – and lo and behold what – who would've thought this would happen in our society – no one is prepared to make the first move – what a shocker – not that i gave a fuck about all that i'm just putting it out as background information – the consequences of all this inactivity is this man – this man here – must act on his own – take the initiative – save his own soul and that – so yes to answer your question again – yes it must be in fuckin public – the floor is yours |
| **Ian** | you know my name |
| **Jimmy** | i might do – say it out loud though |

31

| | |
|---|---|
| **Ian** | my name is ian gibson – i am fifty-two years old – in nineteen seventy-four i was sixteen |
| **Jimmy** | so was i |
| **Ian** | i know that |
| **Jimmy** | you look younger than me – life done you less damage – maybe i'm just a fuck up – don't think that sayin we were both sixteen in nineteen seventy-four makes us the same – it doesn't |
| **Ian** | we've seen the same things |
| **Jimmy** | you don't know what the fuck i've seen – say it – that's what you're here to do so fucking do it – say it – out loud – every fucking detail – i'll start you off – on the third of july nineteen seventy-four . . . |
| **Ian** | on the third of july nineteen seventy-four . . . |
| **Jimmy** | you don't know the start of the story – you only know the start of your fucking story – i'll start – on the third of july nineteen seventy-four poland – you hear that robert – poland |
| **Robert** | we nearly scored there – what's the fucking point in nearly scoring |
| **Jimmy** | poland were playin germany in the world cup – in this pub – this very pub – five men an the barman – were watchin the match – the reason i know they were watchin the match was because they were watchin it on our tv – there was no tv in the bar back then – so my da took the tv from our house an carried it up the street |

to the pub – so he could have a pint an
watch the match at the same time – much
the same as we're doing now – he had
backed poland to win the world cup – we
only had one tv – everybody only had one
tv – there was murder in our house that
day – excuse the pun – whenever my da
said he was takin the tv my ma threw a
wobbler – a lot of screamin an shoutin –
normal behaviour – anyway my da took
the tv an carried it up the street to the pub
– my ma ran behind him an threw his     `
dinner after him – last thing she said to
him was – stay up there – live up there if
you want – she didn't mean that it was just
the type a thing she used to say – just
before he left the house with the tv he
shouted up the stairs to me if i wanted to
come up with him to watch the match – it
was the first time he had ever asked me if i
wanted to go to the pub with him – not to
drink – just to be in his company – i was
too busy sittin in my room thinkin about
this girl i wanted to go out with called
jackie – so i said no – maybe later – and
my ma shouted he's never going out with
you – so five punters a barman a tv and the
poland and germany match – my da knew
all these men a lifetime – all grew up an
lived in the same area – they were like a
wee community of their own – all catholics
– thinkin back on that now i don't know
what that means – ya think of a catholic as
a certain thing – well i don't know what
opinions any of these men had – don't know
what opinions my da had – he never spoke

of such things – so for the purposes of this
story they were just catholics – at the time
i wouldn't have known their ages – when
you're sixteen all men look like men –
difficult to tell – they all looked old – they
all looked older than you think you're ever
going to reach – i know their ages now –
my da was forty-six married with one child
– me – he worked in the fruit market –
liked a drink an the odd bet – got married
to my mother when they were both
nineteen – another man – who also worked
in the fruit market was fifty-three – he was
married with six children – i went to
school with two of his sons – forty-eight –
a joiner – not married – lived with his
mother – fifty-six – worked in the civil
service – married – three grown-up
children – can't remember think they all
lived in different parts of the world – thirty-
six – not married – teacher – any time ya
saw him at the weekend he was drunk –
always remember him bein very well
dressed – rumour had it he was a bit odd –
and the barman – thirty-nine – married with
twin babies – combined age – two hundred
and seventy-eight years old – two hundred
and seventy-eight years of living – they
lived in the same area – they drank in the
same pub and knew nearly everythin about
each other – two hundred and seventy-
eight years – one mother – four wives –
and then all those children – that's what
we're talkin about here – that's the story –
so – they're watchin the match on our tv –
pints in hand – and – what – yer turn

| Ian | is that it – is this the way we're going |
|---|---|
| Jimmy | yer turn |
| Ian | i have to tell this my own way |
| Jimmy | just start |
| Ian | i was sixteen |
| Jimmy | we know that |
| Ian | let me say what i have to say |
| Jimmy | just say what happened – simple enough isn't it – the facts are the truth – isn't that why you're here to tell the truth and be reconciled |
| Ian | no – and there's more to the truth than facts – i just didn't decide to do what i did there and then – i had lived a life up to that point |
| Jimmy | yer life isn't an excuse |
| Ian | it can help explain |
| Jimmy | i don't need an explanation – i get it – we were – are – fenian bastards – and our existence threatened the state – we were – are – the enemy – you were at war with us – all of us – we were all potential members of the ira an therefore legitimate targets – you were told that and you believed it – but most of all you were told we were fenian bastards – i know that because twenty thousand protestants marched by the top of our street on the way to a vanguard rally – maybe you were one of them |
| Ian | i was – as was my father |

35

| | |
|---|---|
| **Jimmy** | well then ya know – twenty thousand people screamin fenian bastards – so as i say i get it – this isn't about why – this is about admitting – here – now |
| **Ian** | i was sixteen years of age when i became a member of the uvf |
| **Jimmy** | my grandfather lied about his age to go an fight in the first world war – he was sixteen – not the same thing though is it |
| **Ian** | i was told it was |
| **Jimmy** | an irish catholic fightin in the british army |
| **Ian** | it's complex – i get that – just let me say what i have to say or at least fuckin start it – up to that point i hadn't been on active service – as kids we were asked to do stuff an we all did it without question |
| **Jimmy** | stuff |
| **Ian** | army drill – cleanin guns – hidin guns – actin as lookouts – ya know what a mean |
| **Jimmy** | yes |
| **Ian** | if there's a picture you have in yer head of me make sure it's when i was sixteen – i was approached not by another sixteen-year-old but by men – grown men – men i had been taught to believe – when i was asked it felt like these men had personally given me an identity – an that now my identity would automatically have respect – it was a war and you were fightin for yer country – the day this happened – third of july nineteen seventy-four – i had only been told the day before what i was goin |

36

to do – i was excited and petrified at the
same time – anyway – i didn't eat – my
mum made me breakfast but i didn't eat it
– i had to meet up with the guy who was
going to drive the car – i was too young to
drive the car – i didn't know him – i was to
meet him an another guy i did know at
four o'clock – i had been given some
money for my birthday – which had been
two weeks before – i went into town and
bought a pair of wranglers – went through
the barriers – soldiers searchin me – i hated
that – being searched in my own city – i
hated how the ira had destroyed my city –
i never felt that i was on the same side as
the soldiers though – they always felt
foreign to me – as if they didn't know why
they were here an what they were fightin
for – bought the wranglers an went home –
had a big row with my mum

**Jimmy**    where was yer da that day

**Ian**    my dad was dead

**Jimmy**    blown up – shot – what

**Ian**    died of a heart attack when he was forty-
three – smoked like a train – inside our
house was always a shitty brown colour
with the smoke – what i learned i learned
on the street not in the house – my parents
were decent people

**Jimmy**    so were mine

**Ian**    i had a big row with my mum – i wanted
her to turn the jeans up but she wouldn't –
turn them up just below the knees like

37

| | |
|---|---|
| **Jimmy** | the seventies |
| **Ian** | aye – she said she couldn't understand that – that it was a waste of material – why would ya buy a new pair a jeans an just cut half a them away – i told her that's what everybody did – she then said to me that's the exact reason why you shouldn't do it – i kept goin on an on an on at her – a was thinkin about goin out that night an wanted to wear the new wranglers – i tortured her until she gave in – for the first year i was in jail she wouldn't come up an see me – disgraced – she came up regular after that but never got used to it – meet up at four o'clock in one of the flats the uvf used – the two other guys would've been in their late twenties – don't ask me anythin about them – i won't tell you |
| **Jimmy** | i wouldn't expect you to – nor do i care |
| **Ian** | the other guy was to drive the car and i was to throw the bomb – the plan was if there was a lookout at the pub just throw it in the doorway without leaving the car – if there was no lookout get out a the car open the door an throw it into the pub – whenever the guy said that i immediately hoped there was a lookout – the other two guys knew each other – i sort of only knew one a them – he was higher up the ranks – it was him that got me involved in the first place – he was from our area – the other guy was from another part of belfast – don't know where – after we knew what we were doin they talked away to each other – sort of ignored me – they smoked a |

lot a fegs – i didn't smoke – i think if i
had've smoked the might have involved me
more in their talk – talkin about football –
the world cup – one a them fancied
holland to win it the other one fancied
west germany – after the guy i knew left
me an the other guy just sat there – wasn't
that long anyway – he smoked another
three or four fegs – then we got into the
car – can't remember any of the journey –
no details – nothing – no idea how long it
took – all i remember is it was still
daylight – the sun was shining – the car
pulled up outside the pub – there was no
lookout – all the guy drivin the car said
was – hurry up to fuck – i had the bomb in
my hand – i got out of the car – he said –
throw it in then run like fuck to the car –
he then drove to the other side a the street –
he didn't want to be near it if it went off
before it should've – i ran across the
pavement – opened the door to the pub –
shouted – shouted – fuckin fenian bastards
– threw the bomb into the bar then ran –
the car moved off before i could get to it –
it turned a corner – i ran after it – i heard
the explosion but didn't look back – the
car stopped – i got in – yer man said –
fuckin yes – fuckin yes – good lad – we
drove off – six men were killed in that
explosion – including your father

| Jimmy | when you opened the door what did ya see |
| Ian | i can't remember |
| Jimmy | what did you fucking see |

| | |
|---|---|
| **Ian** | fenian bastards – nothing but fenian bastards |
| **Jimmy** | a group of men having a drink and watching a football match – where were they sittin – in this bar – the one we are sittin in now – where were they sittin – (*Moves to centre stage.*) – the bar was here – (*Points upstage.*) – you ran in through the door there – (*Points downstage.*) – when you ran in the bar would've been directly in front of you – where were they sittin |
| **Ian** | the barman was behind the bar – two men were sittin at opposite ends of the bar – the other three were closer to the tv set – which was in the middle of the bar |
| **Jimmy** | where did you throw the bomb |
| **Ian** | i threw it at the three men watchin the tv – i had been told it was always best to try an hit the middle – it spreads out in all directions – do more damage – there was only six men in the bar – all dead |
| **Jimmy** | say their names – do you know their names |
| **Ian** | yes – joe turner |
| **Jimmy** | the barman – (*Moves to where the bar was.*) – standin here servin drink – doin his job – say all their names at once – like a group – this is about us livin through this together – isn't that why you're here – both sixteen |
| **Ian** | joe turner – aiden miskelly – paddy mallon – frank healy – brendan mcguigan – an john loughrin |

| Jimmy | joe behind the bar – aiden and brendan at either end of it – paddy frank – and my da – sittin round the tv – all watchin poland play west germany in the world cup – that's just a picture though isn't it – that's not the story – we don't know the story – no one left to tell us – i always like to think that it ended with a joke an a laugh – men havin a drink to help them ease the burden of the daily grind – an on top of that – belfast in those days – a few drinks – a release – watchin the match an shootin the shit – maybe like they were in their own cave or somethin – protected from all the fuckin nonsense goin on in the outside world – the only thoughts bein about who's going to win – an what awaits me when i walk in through the door with the tv – is it goin to be the silent treatment or the screamin match – either way it was worth it – say for that moment in time – for that evening – that's all they wanted |
|---|---|
| Ian | i'm here – but i don't know what to say to you |
| Jimmy | you could start with i'm sorry |
| Ian | i can't speak for the actions of a sixteen-year-old child – but i can speak for myself now – i'm sorry what happened |
| Jimmy | that's of no use |
| Ian | i know |
| Jimmy | no you don't |
| Ian | i think i do |

| | |
|---|---|
| Jimmy | maybe we should travel back in time – one sixteen-year-old kid sayin they're sorry to another |
| Ian | i wouldn't have said it then |
| Jimmy | i wouldn't have listened |
| Ian | and you are now |
| Jimmy | bein sorry has no meaning – i don't know what sorry is – is it you sayin if you had to to it all again you wouldn't |
| Ian | it means now as a man – ian gibson feels that what he did as a sixteen-year-old kid was wrong – and wasn't worth it |
| Jimmy | if i believed in god i'd say it's him that deals in right an wrong |
| Ian | i didn't have to come here |
| Jimmy | yes you did |
| Ian | maybe it's just about talking |
| Jimmy | talking |
| Ian | yes – and listening |
| Jimmy | i'll tell you what happened – haven't ever told this to anyone – strange that the first person i tell it to is you – i heard the same explosion you heard – i knew where it was right away – used to the sound of explosions in those days – knew how close they were – knew it was at the top a the street – only place worth blowing up at the top a the street was the pub – my mum knew where it was as well – she was out a the house an up the street in one stride – |

her screamin would've woken the dead – it
didn't though – i walked up the street –
too frightened to run – everyone movin
past me – it felt like i was movin in slow
motion – i knew – before i got there i knew
– that's what happens here – men go out
for a pint an the end up blown up or shot
– there's no way that wasn't going to be
the case – a rule of nature – a law of
belfast – it was mayhem – it was like the
whole a the world had landed on yer
doorstep – everyone tryin to control
somethin that was beyond control – the
whole front a the pub had been blown
away – so ya could see inside – didn't
make much difference everythin inside had
been blown outside – includin the people –
joe turner had a shaft of glass the length of
a sword through his chest – aiden
miskelly's legs had been blown off an
brendan mcguigan looked untouched –
they were dead – you just knew they were
dead – paddy frank and my da were
nowhere to be seen – for a moment i
thought maybe my da wasn't there – or
maybe they had disappeared into thin air –
an the would reappear once everythin had
settled down – maybe my da had a super
power that i didn't know – he had the
ability to disappear when it looked like the
end was near – he didn't have a super
power but he did disappear – there was
nothin of him left – my mother was holdin
his coat – she must've seen it in the rubble
– she was lookin around the spot where
she found the coat – i saw somethin her

eyes hadn't reached yet – my dad's trousers
– one of his legs still in them – i could see
my mum's look gettin closer to the trousers
– i ran towards her – there was a priest
there he tried to stop me – i pushed him
away – i was too late – she stopped
screaming – she just kept repeating the
same words – oh john – oh dear god john
– she held me tight to her thinkin she was
shieldin me from it – both of us too late –
both saw what we shouldn't have – bits an
pieces – it was all just bits an pieces – if
you had've hung around that's what you
would've seen

| | |
|---|---|
| **Ian** | i've also seen things i shouldn't have |
| **Jimmy** | was i responsible for them |
| **Ian** | no |
| **Jimmy** | then that's not for now is it – so what did you do – we were both sixteen – i've told you what i did – so what did you do after you drove off – how did you celebrate |
| **Ian** | that isn't part of this |
| **Jimmy** | just say it – finish the story |
| **Ian** | it's not a story it's a life experience |
| **Jimmy** | they teach you that bullshit in jail – it's one fucking story among thousands – so have the decency to finish it |
| **Ian** | we drove to some waste ground left the car there an some wee lads torched it – the type a thing i did when i was fourteen – we both went round to a social club near by – |

to report back – the two of us walked
there in silence – the other guy wasn't
silent because he was thinking about what
had just happened – he was all pumped up
– i think he just couldn't be bothered
talkin to me because i was a kid – what
had just happened bonded us and the walk
to the social showed we were strangers –
when we got into the place it was bunged

**Jimmy**      did the all cheer

**Ian**        those that knew what had happened did –
most a the people were there just because
it was a club ya could get cheap drink in –
the top man bought me a pint – i didn't
drink – i didn't say that – just drank – the
other guy gave him all the details – talk
about doin a good job – fightin the good
fight – felt good to hear that – i was a
soldier that had played his part in the
battle against republicanism – i was a
soldier – younger than the british soldiers
on the street but a soldier none the less –
i was told there would be other things to
do but for the while i had to stay low –
another pint – my head was spinnin – part
pride part fear part drink – the top man
then pointed me to a group of girls in the
corner – all a bit older than me – he said
they were doin their bit – he said i could
have any one a them i wanted – only i
had the pints in me i wouldn't have had
the courage to go over to talk to them – i
sat with them – there was a few other
boys there – older than me – the girls were
all interested in me though – the older boys

|       |                                                                                          |
|-------|------------------------------------------------------------------------------------------|
|       | knew not to say anythin – i talked with a girl called sheila                             |
| Jimmy | what about                                                                               |
| Ian   | we had both gone to the same school – she didn't remember me – i remembered her though – she kissed me an we went outside |
| Jimmy | that was yer reward                                                                      |
| Ian   | yeah – it was the first time i had sex – up an entry – she got pregnant                   |
| Jimmy | some fuckin circle of life that – does the child know how it came about                  |
| Ian   | no                                                                                       |
| Jimmy | you should tell them – add some colour to their life experience                          |
| Ian   | fuck up – right – that's enough – just shut the fuck up                                   |
| Jimmy | sorry i have no right to talk about yer child                                            |
| Ian   | she had an abortion – i didn't know that at the time – didn't know anythin about it at all – i knew that wee girl but didn't – so i didn't see her again after that – a couple a years ago i'm standin in this bar an this women comes over to me – asked me did i remember her – drunk like – both drunk – i didn't remember – she told me who she was – i remembered then alright – told her i was sorry i was only a kid – then she told me about the abortion – had to go to england to get it done – her an her friend – |

|        |                                                                 |
|--------|-----------------------------------------------------------------|
|        | got the boat to liverpool – got it done – then got the boat back – never told anyone – too ashamed – she said to me that night – that group a girls – they were all warned whatever one i picked had to do what i wanted – told me it all haunted her – and that's how she looked – haunted |
| Jimmy  | not much of a reward then after all |
| Ian    | stop saying stupid fucking things – there's no point in this if it doesn't fuckin mean something |
| Jimmy  | don't ask me to feel sorry for you – i don't |
| Ian    | i'm not asking for that – that doesn't mean it didn't happen – it doesn't mean it's not a part of my life – i'm no less or no more alive than you are |
| Jimmy  | what else did you do then – what other events are part of your life – the aftermath – what did you become – moulded – shaped – formed – the consequences of yer actions |
| Ian    | i went to jail |
| Jimmy  | i know that |
| Ian    | educated myself while i was in ther |
| Jimmy  | what did you educate yerself to be |
| Ian    | i've a degree in . . . |
| Jimmy  | don't tell me any more – i thought i needed to know who you are – what has happened to you in yer life – might explain somethin – the truth of the matter is i don't care – i don't hate you – i just don't care – maybe |

|       |                                                                                 |
|-------|---------------------------------------------------------------------------------|
|       | i needed to see you face to face to understand that – i need to tell you how things are for me though |
| **Ian** | right |
| **Jimmy** | no not like that – not to punish you – you can leave any time you want – i'm just letting you know what you're up against – with the others maybe – if you choose to meet them – if they allow you to meet them – just in case |
| **Ian** | i understand |
| **Jimmy** | you don't – that's the point |
| **Ian** | my actions have consequences – what do you think this is about |
| **Jimmy** | i can't do anything about that – i don't care – you do care or at least think you do or else you wouldn't be here – i didn't go to university – either inside or outside jail |
| **Ian** | you were in jail – where |
| **Jimmy** | no – that's not happening – i'm not giving you that way out – help you by saying i was really one of the enemy – bond – swap jail stories – no – it doesn't matter what i may or may not have done – you killed my father not me – i had just finished my o levels that summer an was plannin to go back an do my a levels – that was always expected of me – when you're an only child there's time spent on you – that's it you see time spent – anyway – i was bright – the expectation was i would go to university – i didn't – i left school at |

48

sixteen an became a spark – that was the
first time i let my mother down – ya don't
know what yer parents mean to each other
when you're growin up – don't see them in
that light – there's somethin happened that
i need to say – whenever my father died i
stopped believin in god – that feels like a
natural response to that – how could
somethin as terrible as that happen an
there still be a god – not believin in god
because of anger has now turned to
atheism – which i'm glad about but it has
consequences – my belief there is no god
an therefore no afterlife began after you
had blown my father up – they are directly
linked – if that incident hadn't have
happened i might still believe in god to this
day – that's important – i didn't know how
this affected my mother – all i really knew
about was how it affected me – all that
time they spent together – they were
married twenty-seven years when he died –
eleven years of that twenty-seven they were
on their own – then sixteen of it with me –
difficult to describe bein an only child to
people who have brothers or sisters – it's
like the three of you are this unit – it
makes sense – it's like ya go through the
world together – yet because there's only
three you still remain individuals – very
close then apart – very close then apart –
the point is that i hadn't realised that they
loved each other – was only a kid – didn't
know what that type of love was – know
it now – married once an have kids of my
own – too late knowin it now though – so

i didn't know how much pain my mother
was in – only knew my own pain – only
child – selfish – i'm not talkin about right
after it by the way – for a year or so she
depended on the women around her – then
as shit started to happen to them they
looked after their own grief – she wanted
me to look after her and i didn't – i looked
after myself – i thought she didn't handle
it well – i felt she didn't try hard enough –
she let grief and loneliness consume her –
the grief and loneliness of havin someone
you love taken away from you for no
reason that you truly understand – she
lived on her own for seventeen years after
my da died – never met another man and
as each year passed gathered up more
illness – never away from the doctor's
surgery – i told her it was all in her head –
that she needed to live life – she needed to
realise that she was on her own but that
that was ok – don't get me wrong we got
on – it was just that i was of no use to her
– i was on my own downward spiral – not
that that's any a yer business – i'm not
lookin for pity here – she wanted me to
notice her and i didn't – she took ill – it
was more serious than a thought – it was
more serious than i would let her believe –
brought into hospital for tests – she had
cancer – i think she got it from worryin –
needed an operation – had the operation
the next day – she died on the operating
table – i didn't get a chance to talk to her –
since the day and hour she died i wanted
to say to her – i'm sorry i didn't notice

what was happening to you – i should've
known better – i should've looked after you
– and you see i can't even put that in a
prayer now – after all this time i can't hear
my father's voice any more – it's gone from
my head – that time has passed – i can still
hear my mother's though – there's nothing
you can do about that – nothing you can
say – nothing you can do

**Ian**     i was sixteen years of age – i'm trying to
do the right thing

**Jimmy**   i know – when the twenty thousand of you
marched by the top of our street i
screamed at the top of my voice – fuckin
orange bastards – fuckin orange bastards –
i was sixteen as well – i know what world
you lived in

*Ian finishes his pint.*

**Robert**  another

**Ian**     no

*Ian stands up and offers Jimmy his hand.
Jimmy stands. They shake hands.*

**Jimmy**   don't ever come back here

*Ian exits. Robert pulls Jimmy another pint
and they watch the match. Poland score.*

**Robert**  yes yes yes – northern ireland my arse

**Jimmy**   that's it over – it's over

**Robert**  it's not over until it's over

**Jimmy**   it's over

**Robert**  you don't care anyway

| | |
|---|---|
| **Jimmy** | i do now it's getting to the end – if i have a choice i'd rather northern ireland win than poland – it would make no sense me wantin poland to win |
| **Robert** | shut up – you talking is going to stop them scoring a goal |
| **Jimmy** | is that how it works |
| **Robert** | i'm concentrating on them getting another goal which might help – you talking is stopping me concentrating |
| **Jimmy** | i'll concentrate on the referee blowin the whistle then |
| | *Silence.* |
| **Robert** | go on – go go |
| **Jimmy** | blow the fuckin whistle |
| | *The final whistle.* |
| **Robert** | jammy bastards |
| **Jimmy** | see what happened there |
| **Robert** | what |
| **Jimmy** | i didn't really concentrate on the referee blowin the whistle but he blew it anyway |
| **Robert** | not the same thing |
| **Jimmy** | no – maybe not |
| **Robert** | what does that mean for the group |
| **Jimmy** | no idea |
| **Robert** | you sit there and watch all the matches but you don't know the overall story |

| | |
|---|---|
| Jimmy | correct |
| Robert | what's the point in that |
| Jimmy | passes the time |
| Robert | you going to meet with that guy again |
| Jimmy | no |
| Robert | i heard what you were talking about |
| Jimmy | you were meant to – no point in it just being me and him – has to be someone else there to pass the story on |
| Robert | is that why you watch the matches – sit in the same pub your dad sat in – watching football |
| Jimmy | i sit and watch matches here because i live round the corner and it's borin watchin them on yer own |
| Robert | i thought you didn't care about the matches |
| Jimmy | it's better than watchin nothing |
| Robert | maybe you should meet him again |
| Jimmy | why |
| Robert | why not |
| Jimmy | why not – because i have no need to – that's why not |
| Robert | some good might come from it |
| Jimmy | you know nothing do you – some good did come from it – we met – we understand each other – that's enough |

*Jimmy finishes his pint.*

| | |
|---|---|
| **Robert** | you want another one |
| **Jimmy** | nah – enough's enough – good luck |
| **Robert** | good night jimmy – see you tomorrow – jammy bastards |
| **Jimmy** | even with god on yer side you can't win – tomorrow |

*Jimmy exits. Robert turns the TV off. He receives a text.*

i mightn't wait up – the baby has me knackered

no problem

don't walk home in case there's trouble

i won't

night

night

*He sits at the bar. He sends a text.*

how are u?

i want to go back to poland – you've abandoned me

don't talk about going home this will work out

i sit in this flat alone all day waiting on u – and u don't appear – you go home to yer family – sometimes i want to end it all

i'll come over after work

will u stay the night

maybe

finish early

i'll try

*Robert starts to clear up. The kids in the*
*street start beating on the window*
*shutters. They shout abuse:*

**Voices**     three-two – three-two – fuckin polish
bastard – dirty smelly fuckin bastard – go
back to where you come from and shite in
the street you fucker – polish wanker –
three-two – three-two – three-two

*Robert gets a baseball bat from behind the*
*bar and stands waiting. Lights fade to*
*dark.*